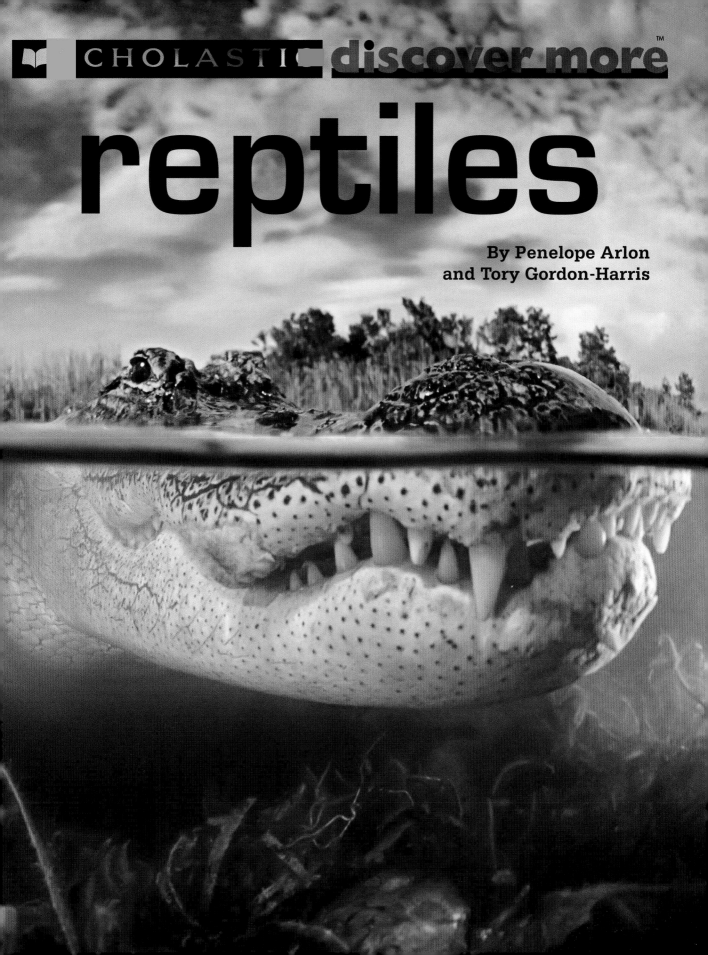

# SCHOLASTIC discover more™

# reptiles

By Penelope Arlon
and Tory Gordon-Harris

# Free digital book

Read real-life stories of reptile attacks, and discover even more about powerful reptile predators!

reptile

attack!

A digital companion to **Reptiles**

**■SCHOLASTIC**

Download your all-new digital book,

## Reptile Attack!

**Log on to**
**www.scholastic.com/discovermore**
**Enter this special code:**

## RC4PMRCRXFWC

## Top five fiercest crocodilians

They all look terrifying, with their big teeth and powerful, muscled bodies, but which are the deadliest crocodilians roaming Earth?

**1 Saltwater crocodile**
The largest living crocodile, these lurk in water and can leap high in the air to grab unsuspecting victims and pull them under.
**Danger rating** 🐊🐊🐊🐊🐊
**Name** Crocodylus porosus
**Length** Average male: 20 ft. (6 m)
**Teeth** 64–68
**Habitat** Northern Australia, eastern India, Southeast Asia

**2 Nile crocodile**
These speedy crocs run at 8.7 mph (14 kph) in bursts and will eat any animals, including big cats! They attack 275 to 745 humans per year.
**Danger rating** 🐊🐊🐊🐊🐊
**Name** Crocodylus niloticus
**Length** Average male: 16.4 ft. (5 m)
**Teeth** 64–68, shaped like cones
**Habitat** Freshwater lakes and rivers in southern and central Africa

**3 American alligator**
Dangerous because they live near humans, these will cross land to find water and may move into swimming pools during droughts.
**Danger rating** 🐊🐊🐊🐊
**Name** Alligator mississippiensis
**Length** 13–14.7 ft. (4–4.5 m)
**Teeth** 72–76
**Habitat** Swamps and rivers in the southeastern United States

**4 Black caiman**
The largest water predators in the Amazon, these have excellent vision and hearing. They live in water but will hunt for prey on land.
**Danger rating** 🐊🐊🐊🐊
**Name** Melanosuchus niger
**Length** Average male: 13 ft. (4 m)
**Teeth** 72–76
**Habitat** Northern South America, especially in the rainforest

**5 Mugger crocodile**
Mugger means "monster" in an Indian language—these are the most dangerous crocs in India. Flat tails propel these superswimmers forward.
**Danger rating** 🐊🐊🐊
**Name** Crocodylus palustris
**Length** 13–16 ft. (3.9–5 m)
**Teeth** 66–68
**Habitat** Southern India, Sri Lanka, Indochina

*You can interact with facts, stats, picture galleries, and videos of the world's deadliest reptiles.*

## Deadly crocodilians

HOME

Only 8 of the 23 crocodilian species are a threat to humans. Every year, hundreds of people die from Nile crocodile attacks in Africa, and that number doesn't even include the many attacks that are not reported. Saltwater crocodiles are responsible for most of the strikes in Asia and Australia. There are around 14 major alligator attacks each year in the United States.

**Attacks stats**

Average number of recorded major attacks per year since 2000

| Crocodilian | Number | Location |
|---|---|---|
| Nile crocodile | 275–745 | Africa |
| American alligator | 11 | Florida |
| Saltwater crocodile | 5 | Australia |
| Saltwater crocodile | 10 | Southeast Asia (2010–2015) |

- See a Nile crocodile
- Top five fiercest
- Alligator attack
- Quick quiz

**Danger**
**How to avoid being eaten!**
- Don't go swimming or wading in water where crocs and gators are known to live.
- In infested water, stay high up on rocks—crocs and gators don't like climbing.
- Run fast and far from a crocodilian. They move quickly, but only in short bursts on land.

**Croc or gator?** Here's how to tell them apart. A croc's top and bottom teeth poke out over its jaws when its mouth is shut.

*You'll be scared and amazed by eyewitness accounts of reptile attacks. There are tips on how to stay safe!*

## Alligator attack

**Date:** Sunday, May 14, 2006
**Place:** Lake George area, Florida
**Crocodilian:** American alligator
**Victim:** A 23-year-old snorkeler

Annemarie Campbell was staying in a cabin in Juniper Wayside Park, in the Ocala National Forest, Florida, with friends. They visited a recreation area not far from Lake George, a popular spot for water sports. While Annemarie was snorkeling, an alligator attacked her. Her friends found her and tried to save her, pulling her from the deadly creature's jaws. Tragically, Annemarie drowned. She had broken ribs, and gashes from the alligator's teeth.

> The people she was staying with came around and found her inside the gator's mouth. They jumped into the water and somehow pulled her out of the gator's mouth.
> —Marion County Fire-Rescue captain Joe Aylsworth

**90%**
of alligator attacks are on people swimming, wading, or at the water's edge.

**The alligator** that attacked Annemarie was 11 feet 4 inches (3.5 m) in length and weighed 407 pounds (184.6 kg). It was later captured and killed.

*It's simple to get your digital book. Go to the website (see left), enter the code, and download the book. Make sure you open it using Adobe Reader.*

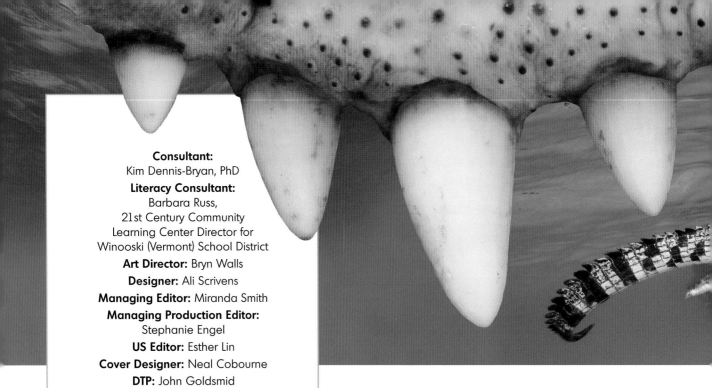

**Consultant:**
Kim Dennis-Bryan, PhD
**Literacy Consultant:**
Barbara Russ,
21st Century Community
Learning Center Director for
Winooski (Vermont) School District
**Art Director:** Bryn Walls
**Designer:** Ali Scrivens
**Managing Editor:** Miranda Smith
**Managing Production Editor:**
Stephanie Engel
**US Editor:** Esther Lin
**Cover Designer:** Neal Cobourne
**DTP:** John Goldsmid
**Digital Photography Editor:** Stephen Chin
**Visual Content Project Manager:**
Diane Allford-Trotman
**Executive Director of Photography,
Scholastic:** Steve Diamond

Library of Congress Cataloging-in-Publication
Data Available

ISBN 978-0-545-50509-3

10 9 8 7 6 5 4 3 2     13 14 15 16 17

Printed in Singapore   46
First edition, July 2013

# Contents

## The world of reptiles

## Snakes and lizards

# The world of reptiles

Reptiles have lived on Earth for at least 300 million years. Over time, they have found some amazing ways to survive in extreme climates. In the Namib Desert in Africa, this web-footed gecko drinks dew from its eyeballs in the early morning.

# What is a reptile?

Reptiles are cold-blooded creatures that are covered in scales. They have lived on our planet for millions of years.

## Carnivores

Most reptiles are meat-eaters, which means that they have to be good hunters. Some are among the most fearsome predators of the animal world.

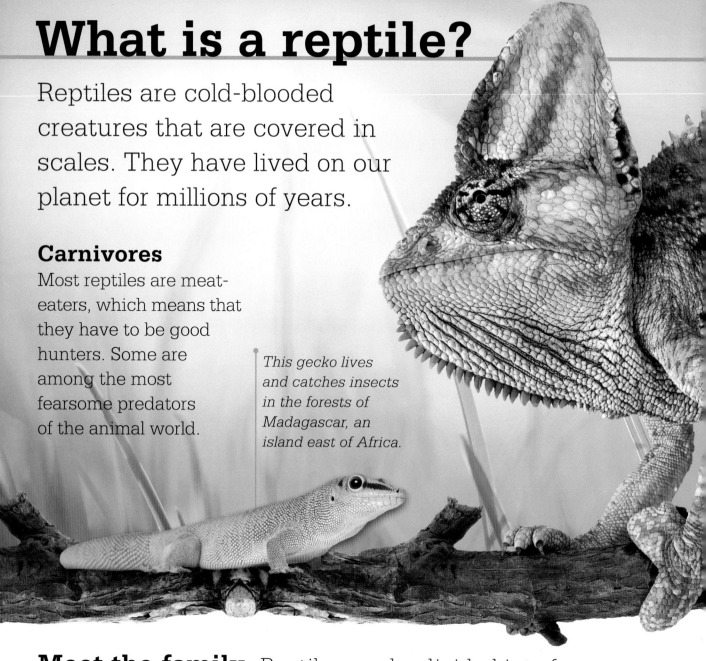

*This gecko lives and catches insects in the forests of Madagascar, an island east of Africa.*

## Meet the family

Reptiles can be divided into four groups.

### Tuataras

The tuatara is the only living member of an ancient reptile group.

### Turtles

These reptiles include tortoises and turtles. They have hard shells.

### Snakes and lizards

These animals have long, flexible bodies. Many of them have forked tongues.

**Nearly all reptiles lay eggs, which hatch babies**

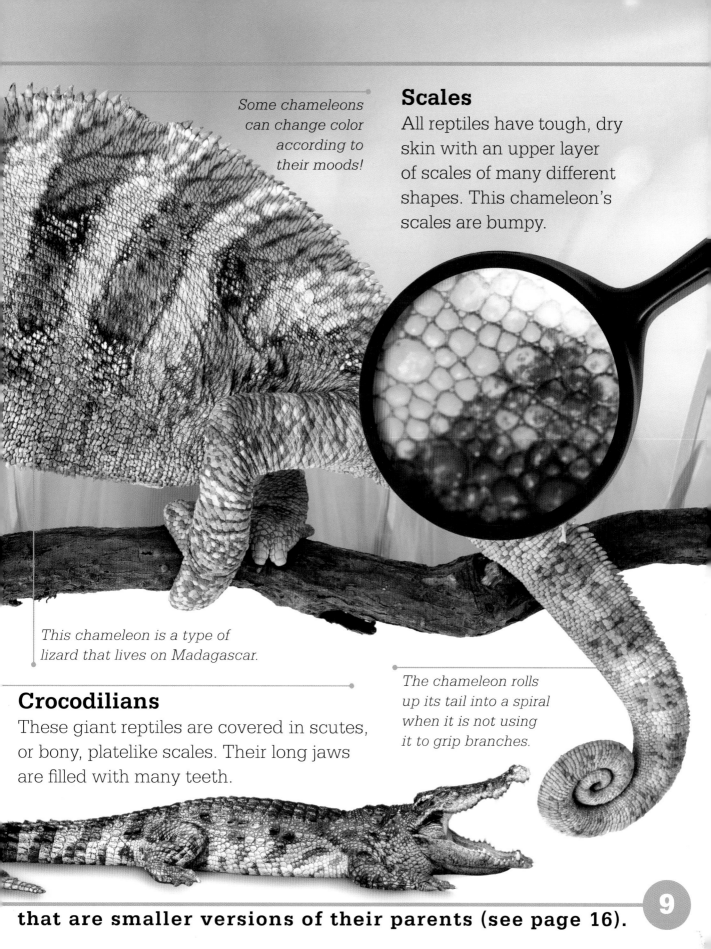

*Some chameleons can change color according to their moods!*

## Scales

All reptiles have tough, dry skin with an upper layer of scales of many different shapes. This chameleon's scales are bumpy.

*This chameleon is a type of lizard that lives on Madagascar.*

*The chameleon rolls up its tail into a spiral when it is not using it to grip branches.*

## Crocodilians

These giant reptiles are covered in scutes, or bony, platelike scales. Their long jaws are filled with many teeth.

**that are smaller versions of their parents (see page 16).**

# Cold-blooded creatures

Reptiles are cold-blooded. This doesn't mean that their blood is cold. It means that their bodies don't automatically control their temperature, like ours do.

## Sunbathing

Reptiles must bask in sunlight to warm their bodies and give them energy. If they are too cold, they cannot move easily or even digest their food.

## Hot enough to hunt

### ❶ Warming up

In the morning, the marine iguana sunbathes to warm up its body after the cool night.

### ❷ Diving in

When the iguana is warm, it dives into chilly water to find food. After ten minutes, it has to return to shore to warm again.

### ❸ Cold and hot

Its body temperature is about 81°F (27°C ) when it emerges from the water. After half an hour in sunlight, its body warms up to 97°F (37°C).

marine iguana

Because reptiles need the heat of the Sun to thrive,

## Hibernation

Winters may be too cold for reptiles. Some, like these garter snakes, survive by hibernating in burrows through the winter.

*Thousands of garter snakes may hibernate together.*

### NEW DISCOVERIES

About 50 new reptiles have been found in the past decade—including some big ones!

This spectacular ruby-eyed green pit viper was discovered in Cambodia in 2011.

It's amazing that it took until 2010 to find this 6-foot-long (1.8 m) Northern Sierra Madre Forest monitor lizard in the Philippines!

they are more common in hot areas of the world.

# Skin and scales

A reptile's skin is covered with scales that act like a suit of armor, protecting the reptile from injury.

## Strong scales

Reptile scales are made of keratin, like your fingernails are, so they are hard but flexible. Reptile skin is waterproof.

*Scales keep insects from biting the reptile.*

## A closer look

**1 Snake**

Most snakes' scales overlap like roof tiles, helping the snake bend easily.

*Scales also protect the animal from damage from surfaces like bark or hot sand.*

**emerald tree boa**

*Waterproof scales help reptiles keep water in their bodies, so they don't have to drink much.*

**Check out the strange,**

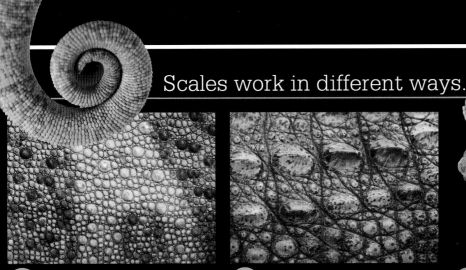

Scales work in different ways.

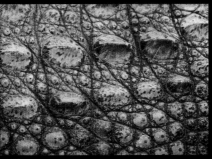

## ② Lizard

Most lizards have small scales with stretchy skin between them. Some are bumpy.

## ③ Crocodile

A crocodile has ridged scutes that are strengthened by bone at their bases.

## ④ Tortoise

The outside of a tortoise shell is shieldlike scutes, fused together.

*Rattlesnakes shake their rattles to frighten predators away.*

*Snakes have no eyelids, so their eyes are also protected by scales.*

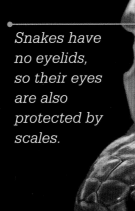

**grass snake**

## Noisy scales

A rattlesnake has large, hollow scales at the end of its tail that it can rattle loudly.

## Skin shedding

Scales can break just like your fingernails do. Reptiles shed their worn-out scales. Most scales fall off in flakes, but snakes slither out of theirs like you would pull off a sock.

spiky scales on the thorny devil on page 20.

# Lying in wait

Many reptiles use camouflage to hide—either from

**Eyes in the sand**

The scales on this sidewinding adder perfectly camouflage it against sand. The snake buries itself with only its eyes showing. When prey passes, it shoots up and delivers a venomous bite into its next meal.

**predators or, like this snake, in order to ambush prey.**

# Eggs

Nearly all reptiles lay eggs, but some snakes and lizards give birth to live young.

*Most turtle shells are round, like Ping-Pong balls.*

## Types of egg

Tortoises and crocodiles lay eggs that have hard shells. Most turtles, lizards, and snakes lay eggs with soft, leathery shells.

*Crocodile eggs look like goose eggs.*

*Soft snake and lizard eggs are often oval.*

*A baby cracks its egg with a special egg tooth on its snout.*

## Underground nests

Most reptiles lay their eggs in burrows underground or under plants, where the temperature remains warm, to keep the eggs healthy.

## Mini-reptiles

Reptile babies all look like miniature versions of their parents.

**ball python**

## Python nest

Most reptiles abandon their eggs after laying them. But the python coils around her eggs, protecting them until they hatch and shivering to keep them warm.

## Live young

Many snakes give birth to live babies. This female garter snake carries between 9 and 12 eggs inside her body, then gives birth to the babies.

## Danger

Reptile babies are very small and can become prey for predators. They are often fierce, and most can move quickly from the moment they hatch.

**Find out more** about alligator moms on pages 58–59.

**baby crocodile hatching**

# Ancient giants

Reptile fossils are constantly being discovered, providing evidence that some of the reptiles of the past were enormous.

## Monster discoveries

Reptiles have been around for at least 300 million years. Prehistoric reptiles were gigantic compared to those of today.

*In 2009, a* Titanoboa *fossil was discovered. It was a colossal, 46-foot-long (14 m) boa that lived 58 million years ago.*

**reticulated python**       **Titanoboa**

*Recent studies show that* Megalania, *a huge lizard that died out 40,000 years ago, was 18 feet (5.5 m) long!*

**Megalania**

**Komodo dragon**

*In 2012, a giant crocodile skull 2–5 million years old was found in Africa. It makes the Nile crocodile look small!*

***Crocodylus thorbjarnarsoni***       **Nile crocodile**

## Prehistoric relatives

By the time of the dinosaurs (between 240 and 65 million years ago), giant reptiles dominated the air and seas. On land, they and the dinosaurs were top predators. The crocodilian relative *Deinosuchus* grew to 50 feet (15 m) long.

Many of the giant reptiles died out with the dinosaurs in a mass extinction 65 million years ago.

**Albertosaurus** ....

**Deinosuchus** .....

Deinosuchus *most likely* preyed on dinosaurs—possibly even Albertosaurus.

**Prehistoric snakes ate baby dinosaurs!**

# Hall of fame

Meet the biggest, the smallest, the most colorful, and some of the weirdest record breakers of the reptile world.

**BIGGEST VENOMOUS REPTILE**
*The Komodo dragon is not just the biggest venomous reptile— it's the biggest venomous animal in the world.*

**WEIRDEST LOOKING**
*The thorny devil is a desert lizard. Its scales carry water from the dewy sand into its mouth.*

**YUCKIEST**
*The horned lizard can squirt blood out of its eyes if it feels threatened!*

**FASTEST REPTILE**
*The spiny-tailed iguana of Costa Rica can run at 22 mph (35 kph).*

**The longest sea journey by any animal was undertaken**

## MOST COLORFUL REPTILE
*The rainbow lizard can be a beautiful red and blue, and it has a striped tail.*

## MOST VENOMOUS REPTILE
*Sea kraits have some of the most toxic venom in the world. Fishermen have to watch out!*

## BIGGEST FANGS
*The Gaboon viper's fangs can be 1.5 inches (4 cm) long.*

dime

## SMALLEST REPTILE
*The Jaragua sphaero is one of the smallest lizards ever found.*

## BIGGEST REPTILE
*Male saltwater crocodiles grow to average lengths of 16 feet (5 m). But some as long as 20 feet (6 m) have been found!*

## LONGEST TONGUE
*Some chameleons have tongues that are twice the length of their bodies!*

by a leatherback turtle. Find out more on page 72.

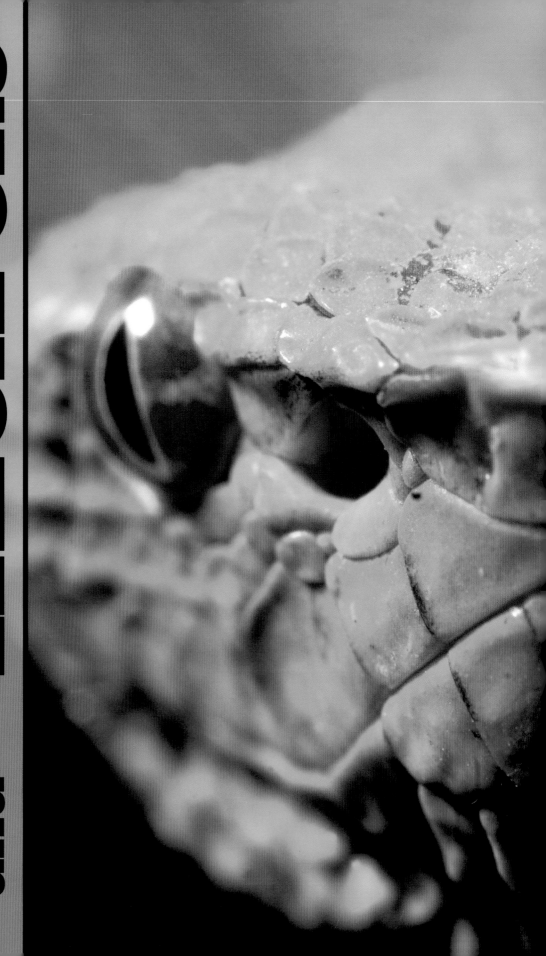

# Snakes and lizards

Snakes and lizards are some of the great hunters of the animal world. This Wagler's pit viper has pits, or holes, between its eyes and mouth. The pits sense the body heat of warm-blooded animals, helping the snake hunt them down.

# Snakes

Many people are afraid of these clever hunters. But only a few snakes are venomous, or use venom to kill.

## Types of snake

### 1 Constrictors

These snakes squeeze their prey to death. They are often large, and include boas and pythons.

carpet python

## Hinged fangs

A viper's fangs lie flat against the roof of its mouth. When the snake strikes, it swings its fangs forward. Venom is squeezed through the fangs.

## FACT ATTACK

### BIGGEST SNAKE

The longest reticulated python ever found was 32 feet (10 m) long. That's almost as long as a school bus!

### SMALLEST SNAKE

The Barbados thread snake is only 4 inches (10 cm) long.

### NEW SPECIES

The Matilda's horned viper was discovered in a Tanzanian forest in 2010 and named after the little girl whose father found it. The red Cambodian kukri snake was discovered in 2012.

eastern diamondback rattlesnake

albino western diamondback rattlesnake

The longest venomous snake is the king cobra. It can

There are four main types of snake.

## 2 Vipers

These venomous snakes have long, hinged fangs. They include adders and rattlesnakes.

## 3 Elapids

Like all venomous elapids, cobras and mambas have fixed fangs, which do not move.

## 4 Colubrids

Two-thirds of snakes are colubrids. Most of them are completely harmless. They include garter, grass, and king snakes.

**Wagler's pit viper**

**Egyptian cobra**

## S-s-s-super senses

Snakes have worse eyesight and hearing than we do, but they have some amazing other senses. They can even pick up the vibrations from moving animals in their jaws!

*When a snake flicks its forked tongue, it is picking up smells.*

▶▶ **Find out more** about venomous snakes on page 34.

*Some snakes have pits beneath their eyes that sense an animal's body heat.*

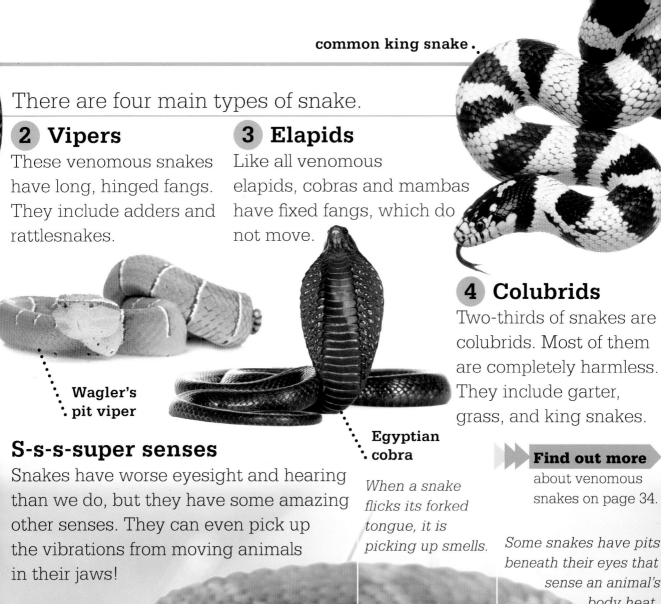

**rear up and look a grown man in the eye.**

# Inside a snake

Beneath the skin covering a snake's long, limbless body, an amazing skeleton and system of organs give this agile predator maximum flexibility.

## Double trouble

Occasionally, snakes are born with two heads! They don't last long in the wild, because they are vulnerable to attack.

*The jawbones move outward when the snake swallows.*

*The backbone is made up of bony segments called vertebrae.*

*The skull bones are loosely connected, so the snake can open wide to swallow large prey.*

*The backbone extends from head to tail.*

*Most of the vertebrae have a pair of ribs attached.*

## Snake skeleton

An incredibly bendy skeleton enables the snake to curl up into an S shape and to wiggle as it moves.

**Find out more** about movement on page 30.

A human has 33 vertebrae and 24 ribs. A snake has up

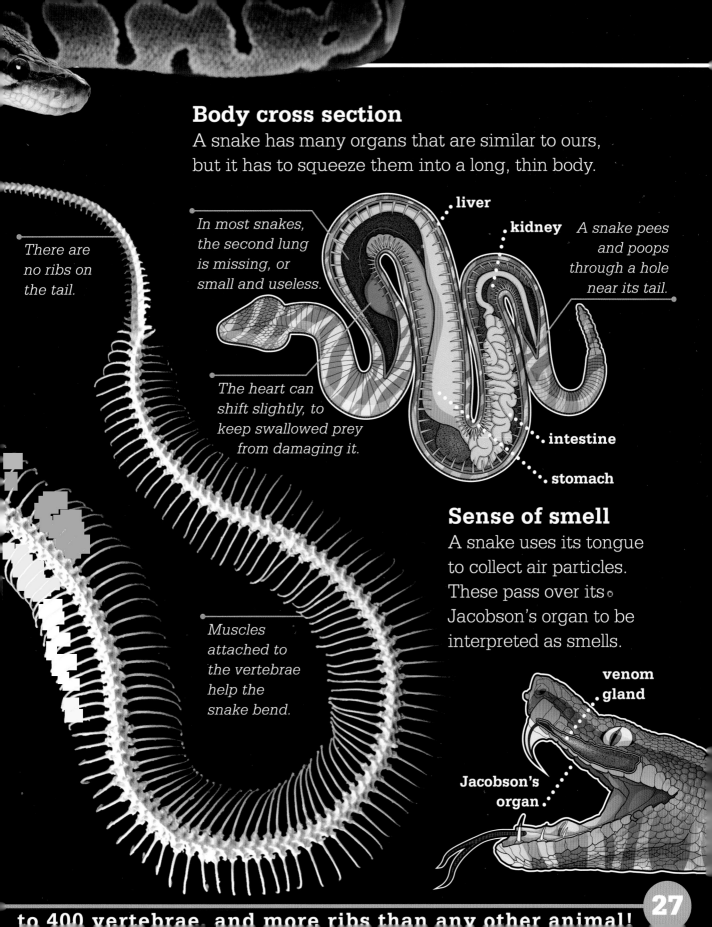

## Body cross section

A snake has many organs that are similar to ours, but it has to squeeze them into a long, thin body.

*In most snakes, the second lung is missing, or small and useless.*

*The heart can shift slightly, to keep swallowed prey from damaging it.*

*There are no ribs on the tail.*

**liver**

**kidney**

*A snake pees and poops through a hole near its tail.*

**intestine**

**stomach**

*Muscles attached to the vertebrae help the snake bend.*

## Sense of smell

A snake uses its tongue to collect air particles. These pass over its Jacobson's organ to be interpreted as smells.

**venom gland**

**Jacobson's organ**

to 400 vertebrae, and more ribs than any other animal!

# A pit of snakes

A snake's colors either help the snake camouflage itself or, when bright, can warn that it is highly venomous.

rainbow boa

emerald tree boa

death adder

blue coral snake

Texas blind snake

leopard snake

carpet python

desert horned viper

rosy boa

European grass snake

brown vine snake

desert horned viper

Burmese python (albino)

rattlesnake

green vine snake

long-nosed tree snake

eastern king snake

gray-banded king snake

leaf-nosed snake

Amazon tree boa

green tree python

golden flying snake

Colorado desert sidewinder

corn snake

Pueblan milk snake

saw-scaled viper

eyelash viper

snow king snake

boa constrictor

Gaboon viper

king cobra

European adder

southern copperhead

green mamba

# Snakes high and low

These agile creatures are some of Earth's most successful animals. They have adapted to every habitat except extreme ice and snow.

black mamba ......

## Treetops to oceans

### Flying snakes

The paradise tree snake glides between trees. It spreads out its ribs to flatten its body into an aerodynamic shape.

### Tree snakes

A tree is a perfect place to hide and observe. This green tree python coils itself around a branch and waits for prey.

young green
tree python ......

*Flying snakes can glide up to 330 feet (100 m).*

golden
flying
snake
......

## Ground snakes

The black mamba lives in the African bush. It is the world's fastest snake—it can slither as fast as a human runs.

## Desert snakes

The sidewinder, a rattlesnake, lives in the desert. It burrows in the sand during the hot day.

## Burrowers

This Peter's thread snake lives underground and has smooth, shiny scales that help it slip through soil.

## Sea snakes

Sea snakes must return to the surface to breathe. This banded sea krait has a paddle-shaped tail to help it swim.

### Snakes everywhere

Snakes live everywhere in the world except in New Zealand, Ireland, Iceland, Greenland, and Antarctica.

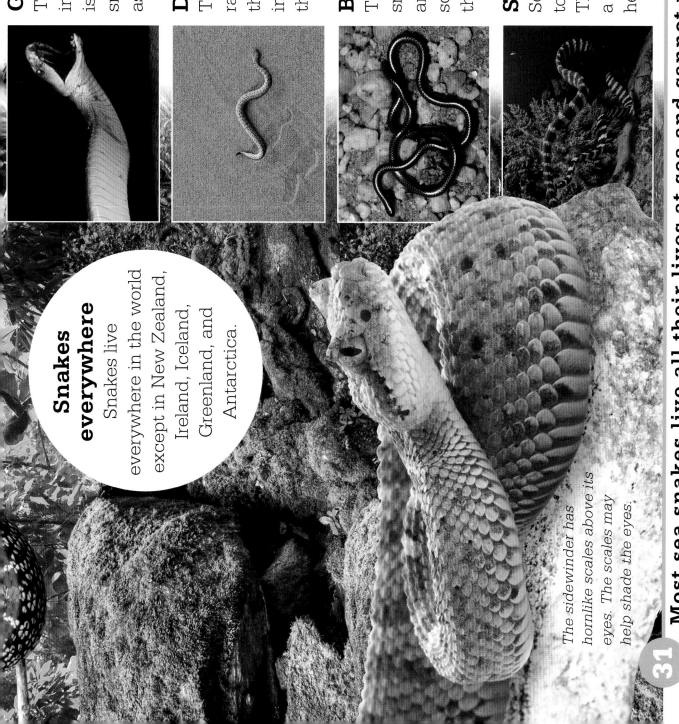

*The sidewinder has hornlike scales above its eyes. The scales may help shade the eyes.*

**Most sea snakes live all their lives at sea and cannot move on land.**

# Snake snacks

All snakes eat other animals, ranging in size from ants to alligators. They even eat one another!

**Massive mouthfuls**
Snakes can separate their jaws, so they can swallow really big animals. Their small teeth help push the prey down.

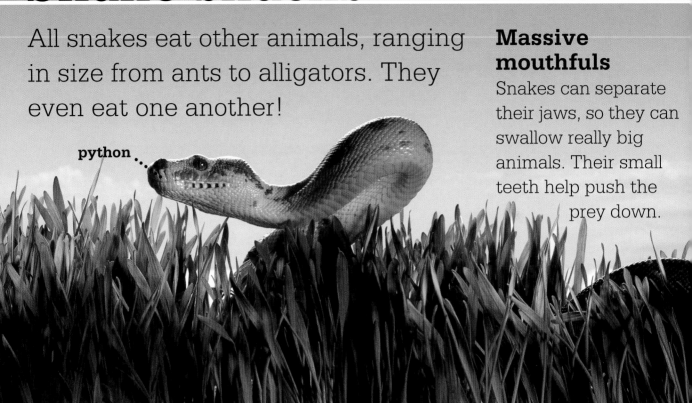

python

**Eating habits** Snakes have some interesting

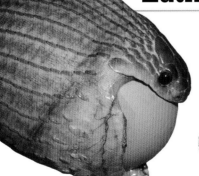

**Egg-eater**
Egg-eating snakes swallow eggs, then spit out the shells.

**Constrictor**
When prey breathes out, a constrictor squeezes a little tighter to suffocate it.

**Rattlesnake**
A rattlesnake's venom contains special poisons so its prey can't stop bleeding.

**Food in a snake's stomach can take up to a couple of**

*The python grabs prey with its mouth, coils itself around the animal, and squeezes. The snake swallows the dead prey whole and headfirst.*

tastes and techniques!

*Birds are attracted to the "worm," and the snake grabs and swallows them.*

## Thread snake

This tiny snake emits a smell to confuse ants so it can steal their larvae.

## Cantil

This snake's tail has a yellow tip that it uses as a lure.

**Find out more** about venomous snakes on page 34.

**months to digest. That's a long time to work on a meal!**

# Snake defense

Although most snakes will flee when threatened, many have excellent backup defenses for emergencies.

**drop of venom**

## Venom

Venom is a toxic saliva that flows down the sharp, hollow fangs of venomous snakes.

## Deadly cobras

Cobras rear up and extend their neck flaps to warn predators. If this doesn't work, most bite, injecting deadly venom that can disable or kill.

**spitting cobra**

*The spitting cobra can shoot venom as far as 6 feet (2 m), into the face of an attacker.*

## Venom can be good!

Venom can be "milked" from snakes. Scientists have recently found out how to separate the toxins for use in medicines.

## Mimicry

The gray-banded king snake pretends to be venomous by copying the coral snake's colors.

# More methods of defense

## Camouflage

You may think it's only a leaf, but look closer and you'll see a perfectly camouflaged Gaboon viper.

## Bright colors

Some lethal snakes, like the coral snake, announce the danger with their bright colors. They would rather warn than waste venom.

## Warning rattle

The venomous rattlesnake warns predators by shaking its loud, rattling tail before striking.

# Ten deadly snakes

Most snakes are pretty harmless, but don't mess with these deadly ones! Lethal snakes are found all around the world, but many of the most venomous live in Australia.

## Top ten

There is much debate about which snakes should be on this list, and what order they should be in. What do you think?

*The ferocious fer-de-lance kills more people with its painful bite than any other reptile in South America does.*

*The eastern diamondback rattlesnake is the most venomous snake in North America. It is responsible for a few deaths every year.*

*Sea snake venom is more toxic than venom from land snakes. One bite from the Belcher's sea snake could kill 1,000 people!*

*The aggressive black mamba of Africa is the fastest snake on Earth. Before antivenin was available, 100 percent of people bitten by mambas died.*

**Don't poke snakes—most will attack if provoked.**

## Antivenin

Luckily, scientists can reverse the effects of snakebites with injections of antivenin.

*King cobras are the most aggressive snakes in the world. Even baby king cobras have full-strength venom.*

**6**

*The saw-scaled viper causes thousands of deaths in India each year.*

**7**

*Tiger snakes live near coastal cities in Australia. They will climb buildings as well as trees.*

**3**

*The eastern brown snake is responsible for about half of all snakebite deaths in Australia.*

**5**

*The death adder of Australia strikes more quickly than any other snake.*

*A bite from the inland taipan of Australia can kill in just 45 minutes.*

**2**

**9**

# Lizards

Chatogekko amazonicus *is less than 1 inch (25 mm) long.*

There are about 3,500 different kinds of lizard living in most habitats, from desert to rainforest, all over the world.

*Most lizards can see in color and have sharp eyesight.*

## Smart designs

Lizards are often shaped to suit their habitats. This Chinese water dragon has sharp claws for gripping branches, and a powerful tail to help it swim.

### FACT ATTACK

**BIGGEST LIZARD**
The largest Komodo dragon found was 10.3 feet (3.1 m) long.

**SMALLEST LIZARD**
The Jaragua sphaero, 0.7 inches (18 mm) long, can fit on a dime.

**NEW SPECIES FOUND IN 2012**
The Anguilla bank skink, a skink with a blue tail, was spotted in the Caribbean. A striped bumblebee gecko was found in Papua New Guinea.

*When this lizard is threatened, it may drop into the water and swim away.*

*Most lizards have four legs, each with five fingers with sharp claws.*

Among lizards, only geckos

## Eye licks

This gecko has no eyelids. It uses its tongue to lick its eyes clean!

*Chameleons have long, sticky, lumpy straight tongues.*

## Tongues

Lizards use their tongues to smell. Their tongues are either forked or straight.

## Legless lizards

The slowworm is often mistaken for a snake because it has no legs. But it has eyelids and ear openings, which snakes don't have.

*Iguanas have straight tongues that they use to feel objects.*

*Monitor lizards flick their forked tongues to taste the air.*

▶▶ **Find out more** about chameleon tongues on page 43.

bearded dragon ........

## Meat-eaters

Most lizards are carnivores, or meat-eaters, and have jaws lined with small, sharp teeth to grab prey.

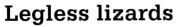

can make sounds: They chirp and click, and one barks!

# Lizard collection

Lizards use their bodies to send messages to one another and to other animals. Some use alarming gestures to frighten or threaten. Others use colors to attract or scare away.

Indo-Chinese forest lizard

Schneider's skink

leopard gecko

fat-tailed gecko

veiled chameleon

flying dragon

closed-litter rainbow skink

green basilisk

blue-tailed skink

lined leaf-tailed gecko

Komodo dragon

web-footed gecko

European green lizard

green anole

crested gecko

agama lizard

Chinese crocodile lizard

broad-headed skink

panther chameleon

green iguana

emerald monitor

panther chameleon

frilled lizard

flying dragon

blue-tongued skink

thorny devil

granite night lizard

pygmy chameleon

Jackson's chameleon

fire skink

midline knob-tail

Gila monster

bearded dragon

tokay gecko

Madagascar day gecko

# Cunning chameleons

If you want to see a really weird lizard, then check out the slow-moving, long-tongued, color-changing chameleon.

panther
..... chameleon

*The tongue reaches slightly above an insect so that the lumpy part lands right on target*

## Eye spy
A chameleon's eyes can move in separate directions! They can also swivel around to see behind it.

*Unlike many other lizards, chameleons have slender but tall bodies.*

*The toes are in two bundles for gripping thin branches.*

*The tail can stretch out like an extra limb and wrap around a branch.*

**One of the biggest**      **chameleons, the Parson's**

## In the mood . . .

Some chameleons can change their skin color depending on mood, light, or temperature.

## . . . to change color

Males may turn bright colors to attract females. An angry one can even turn black with fury!

## Tiny discovery

In 2012, the smallest chameleon in the world, *Brookesia micra*, was found.

*Brookesia micra* . . . . . . . . .

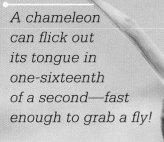

*A chameleon can flick out its tongue in one-sixteenth of a second—fast enough to grab a fly!*

*The Jackson's chameleon grows to about 10 inches (25 cm).*

## Tongue flick

Chameleons mostly eat insects. Instead of running after an insect to catch it, a chameleon shoots out its enormous, sticky tongue and traps the insect.

## Triple horn

The male Jackson's chameleon has three horns on its head, making it look like an ancient dinosaur. It sometimes uses them to push other males away.

**chameleon, can grow to the size of a rabbit.**

# Don't eat me!

Lizards need smart methods of defense to keep their predators from gobbling them up.

*The tail will eventually grow back.*

## Breaking away

If this gecko is grabbed by a greedy predator, it simply breaks off its tail. The tail keeps wriggling to distract the predator while the gecko races off!

## Water sprinter

Basilisk lizards can sprint over the surface of water. Recent studies have shown that they do this by constantly "tripping" and then righting themselves.

## Frightening frill

The frilled lizard has lots of tricks up its sleeve. It hisses, and flares and waves its huge neck frill, then sprints away on its hind legs.

## Leaping and gliding

When threatened, the flying dragon can stretch out huge flaps of skin along its movable ribs and glide up to 25 feet (8 m) from one tree to another.

**The barking gecko arches its back and barks like a dog**

## Disappearing act
Many lizards use camouflage to disappear into the background. This gecko's patchy-colored scales blend beautifully into the rock.

## Look at my tongue!
When it is attacked, the blue-tongued skink puffs itself up, hisses, and sticks out its bright blue tongue!

## Too late!
Some lizards are just not quick or clever enough and are munched up for dinner.

owl eating a lizard

## Watch out!
The horned lizard can squirt blood out of its eyes to surprise predators! The spurts can reach distances of up to 5 feet (1.5 m).

**when it feels threatened!**

# Hairy feet

Geckos are small, agile lizards with very clever feet! They can walk up walls and race across ceilings.

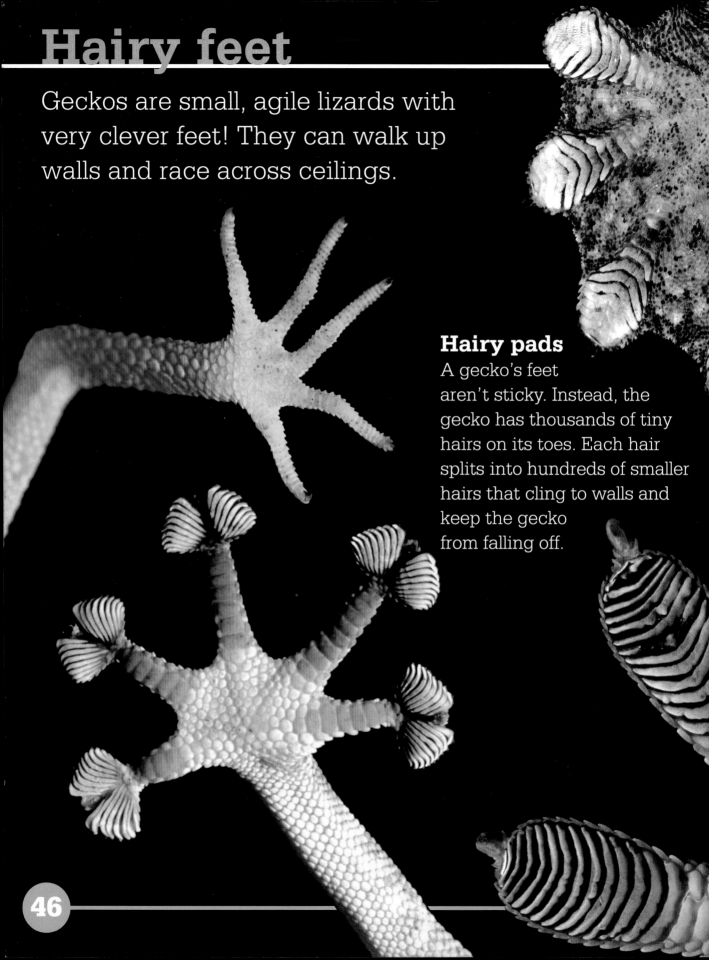

### Hairy pads

A gecko's feet aren't sticky. Instead, the gecko has thousands of tiny hairs on its toes. Each hair splits into hundreds of smaller hairs that cling to walls and keep the gecko from falling off.

Scientists realized only recently how gecko feet work. Some companies are trying to copy this method and make a nonsticky glue!

# Venomous giants

Gigantic lizards roam a small group of islands in Indonesia. Meet the enormous, venomous Komodo dragons.

## Living dragons

Komodo dragons are powerful monitor lizards that average about 8 feet (2.4 m) long. They have huge, muscular tails, and they eat any prey—dead or alive—that they can find.

## Attack-and-wait hunting

### Strike and bite

A dragon waits for prey, such as this buffalo, to pass. It pounces and bites hard, releasing venom through its teeth.

### Tasty rewards

The venom takes some time to work. The dragon follows the prey until it dies, then eats it up.

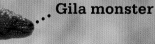

Gila monster

Mexican beaded lizard

## Stay away!

The Gila monster and the Mexican beaded lizard are two other venomous lizards. It is thought that they use their venom for defense, not hunting.

*Claws like daggers grip prey.*

**Komodo dragons use their forked tongues to smell prey.**

## Dragon nests

The female Komodo dragon uses her sharp claws to make a burrow. She lays her eggs inside it and guards the nest for six months, until the eggs hatch.

*Venom runs down grooves on a dragon's teeth when it bites.*

**They can detect a dead animal from 7 miles (11 km) away.**

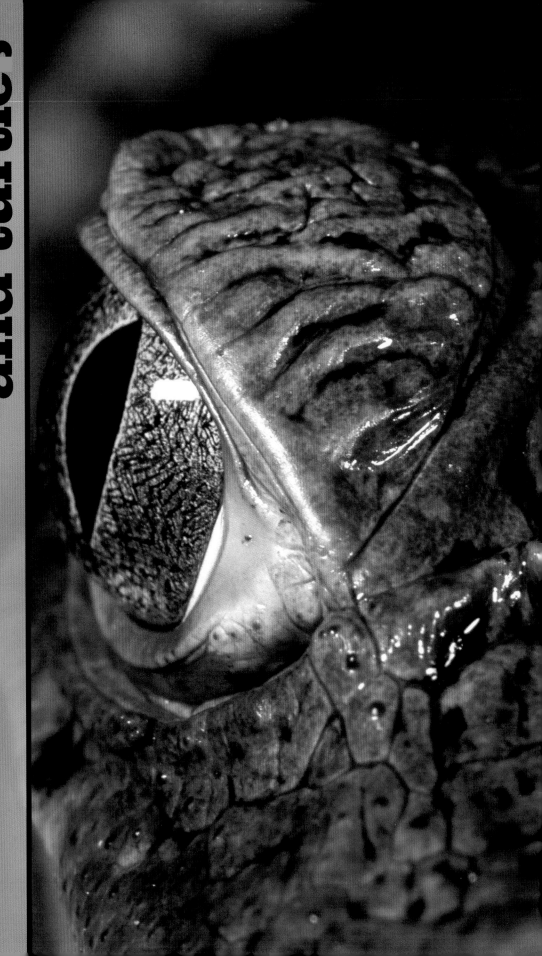

# Crocodilians
## and turtles

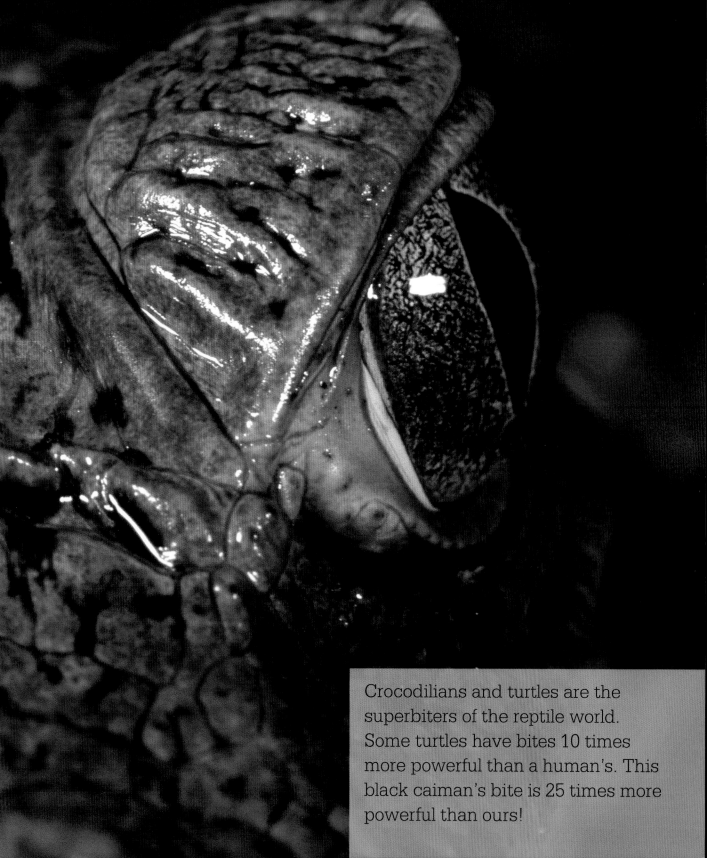

Crocodilians and turtles are the superbiters of the reptile world. Some turtles have bites 10 times more powerful than a human's. This black caiman's bite is 25 times more powerful than ours!

# Crocodilians

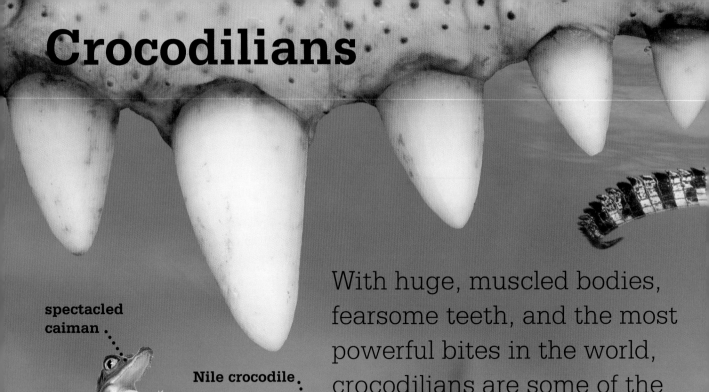

spectacled caiman

Nile crocodile

With huge, muscled bodies, fearsome teeth, and the most powerful bites in the world, crocodilians are some of the most intimidating reptiles of all.

## FACT ATTACK

**BIGGEST CROCODILIAN**
The saltwater crocodile averages 16 feet (5 m) in length.

**SMALLEST CROCODILIAN**
The Cuvier's dwarf caiman, a type of alligator found in South America, is about 4.3 feet (1.3 m) long.

**CROC COPY**
To honor the crocodile, some tribal people in New Guinea scar their skin to match the croc's.

## Useful tail

Crocodilians don't need to eat often. They can eat 23 percent of their body weight in one meal, and they store much of their fat in their huge tails.

## No sweat

Crocodilians can't sweat. They cool off by lying still, with their mouths open.

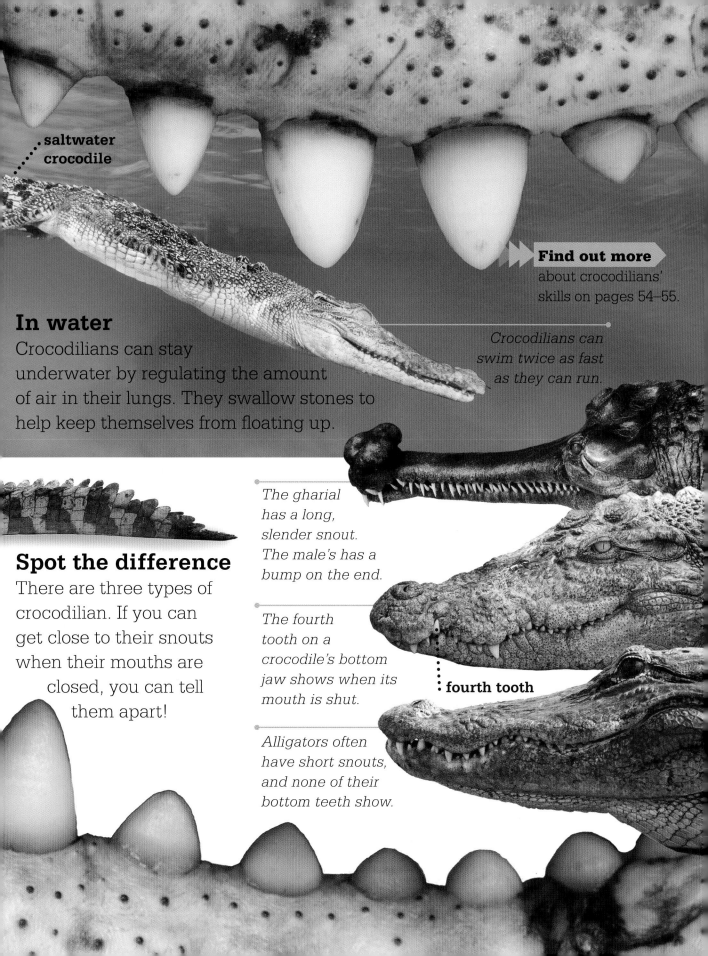

saltwater
crocodile

## In water
Crocodilians can stay underwater by regulating the amount of air in their lungs. They swallow stones to help keep themselves from floating up.

**Find out more** about crocodilians' skills on pages 54–55.

*Crocodilians can swim twice as fast as they can run.*

## Spot the difference
There are three types of crocodilian. If you can get close to their snouts when their mouths are closed, you can tell them apart!

*The gharial has a long, slender snout. The male's has a bump on the end.*

*The fourth tooth on a crocodile's bottom jaw shows when its mouth is shut.*

**fourth tooth**

*Alligators often have short snouts, and none of their bottom teeth show.*

# Super skull

Crocodilians' skulls are perfectly designed for killing. The saltwater crocodile has the strongest recorded bite in the animal kingdom.

*A crocodilian's jaws snap shut very strongly, but the muscles that open them again are relatively weak.*

*The upper and lower jaws are incredibly sensitive to tiny movements in water, enabling the animal to detect its prey.*

## Terrifying teeth

The long snout is packed with supersharp teeth. The teeth often break when the crocodilian grabs prey, but, unlike ours, these teeth are replaced. A crocodilian can go through thousands of teeth in its lifetime!

*Each tooth has hollow roots, with a replacement tooth growing inside.*

**A crocodilian closes off its nostrils and ears when it**

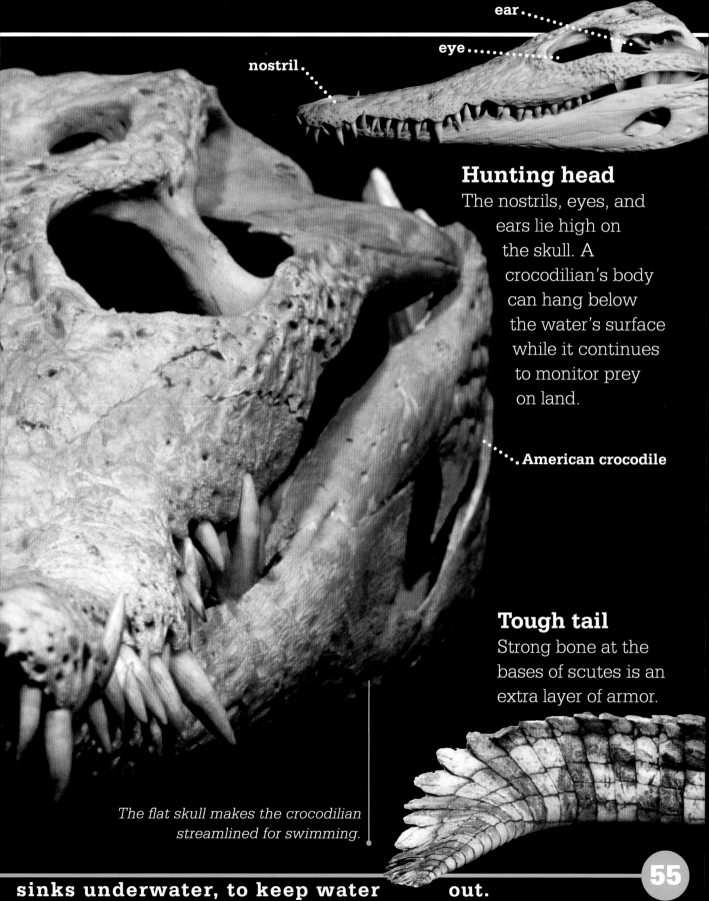

ear ......

eye ......

nostril ......

## Hunting head

The nostrils, eyes, and ears lie high on the skull. A crocodilian's body can hang below the water's surface while it continues to monitor prey on land.

...... American crocodile

## Tough tail

Strong bone at the bases of scutes is an extra layer of armor.

*The flat skull makes the crocodilian streamlined for swimming.*

**sinks underwater, to keep water out.**

# Watch out for the gators!

Travel through the swampy Everglades, in Florida, and you may spot America's biggest predator—the giant American alligator.

## Gator groups

Alligators do not live in packs—they don't rely on one another to survive. But they are often found in big groups, particularly in a good feeding area or in the breeding season.

## Speedy

Alligators are slightly smaller than crocodiles, but they are fast. They can run in short bursts of about 10 mph (16 kph).

*In 2012, a 17-foot-long (5 m) Burmese python was found in Florida with 87 eggs inside her!*

Burmese python

## Gigantic bite

In tests done by very brave scientists, it was shown that the American alligator has one of the animal world's strongest bites.

## Big snakes

In the 1980s, owners released pet pythons into the Everglades because they grew too large for their homes. They are now a huge problem. They attack the wildlife—even alligators.

# Alligator holes

### 1 Hard work

Alligators create their own ponds for the dry season. They dig big holes in the ground with their mouths and claws.

### 2 Private pond

Rain fills the hole, and when the dry season arrives, the alligator is left with its own private pond.

### 3 Easy lunch

Since the pond may be the only water in the area, other animals come there to drink. The gator gets an easy meal!

# Nesting alligators

Most reptiles abandon their eggs. Ferocious crocodilians, however, like these American alligators, are surprisingly good mothers.

## Breeding time

In the spring, American alligators gather to breed. The males bellow, slap the water, and vibrate (as shown here) to attract females.

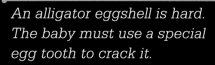

*An alligator eggshell is hard. The baby must use a special egg tooth to crack it.*

## Time to nest

### The nest

Female alligators build nests by scraping up piles of plants and mud.

### Guarding

The alligator doesn't sit on her eggs, but she does watch the nest.

### Hatching

The babies squeak when they are about to hatch, and the mother uncovers the eggs.

**Florida red-bellied turtles sometimes lay their eggs in**

## Baby gators

The mother rolls any unhatched eggs on the roof of her mouth to open them. She carries the babies to a shallow pool, where they swim instinctively.

*Baby alligators are striped, which is good camouflage.*

## On guard

The mother guards her babies for up to a year. They squeal to her when they are in danger.

alligator nests, knowing that they will be looked after!

# The hunt

A crocodilian is not fussy about what animal it eats. It hunts on land and in water, and it will eat practically any animal that crosses its path.

saltwater crocodile

## Saltwater crocodile

The world's biggest crocodile, the saltwater crocodile, swims in lakes, rivers, and the ocean. It hunts fish and turtles. It may even attack a great white shark!

*When the crocodile thrashes around, attacking its victims, a throat flap closes to keep water out.*

**This crocodile can swim three times faster than a**

# Nile crocodile  Top predator

### ❶ The water hole
Nile crocodiles in Africa lurk in rivers or lakes, waiting for prey like antelopes or warthogs to arrive to drink.

### ❷ Attack!
The crocodile grasps the prey in its teeth. If its teeth break, they regrow throughout the croc's life.

### ❸ The kill
The crocodile drowns its prey. It then tears off chunks of meat and swallows them whole.

## The death roll
When a crocodile catches bigger prey, it sometimes grabs the animal and rolls it over in the water to drown it. This is known as a death roll.

## Flick and swallow
A crocodile can't chew—even with all those teeth! Instead, it flips meat to the back of its mouth, opens its throat, and swallows it whole.

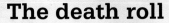

**human can!**

# Turtles

Turtles are easy to spot, because they carry their homes on their backs!

## A watery life

Sea and freshwater turtles have to return to the water's surface to breathe. The females also lay their eggs on land.

### Turtle or tortoise?

We tend to call land turtles tortoises. We call those that live both in freshwater and on land turtles or terrapins. Sea turtles live mostly in the sea.

**red-eared slider**

*The shell is made of bone, covered by scutes that are fused together.*

**Turtles are found in every region of the world except**

## Snapper

The alligator snapping turtle is the largest freshwater turtle in the world. It can grow to lengths of 32 inches (81 cm).

*The turtle has a wormlike pink flap on its tongue that it uses to lure prey.*

**Find out more** about sea turtles on pages 68–69.

*The shell protects the turtle from bumps as well as from hungry predators.*

**leopard
..... tortoise**

## Turtle feet

Tortoises and turtles have different feet. Tortoises have clumpy feet for walking on the ground. Turtle toes are broad for swimming. Sea turtle claws are fused together, forming flippers.

**sea turtle
flipper ..**

**tortoise
foot ...**

**turtle foot ..**

## Eggs

Both tortoises and turtles lay their eggs on land. They lay them safely underground and then leave; the babies take care of themselves after they hatch.

*Turtles have no teeth. Instead, they have hard beaks that can bite and tear food.*

Antarctica.

# Under the shell

A turtle's shell may look hollow, but it acts as armor, protecting all the soft body parts that it contains.

*A turtle can withdraw its head into its shell only if it exhales the air from its lungs. It can hold its breath for a long time!*

## Shell parts

The shell is made of two parts: the carapace (top) and the plastron (underside). They are fused together at the sides, leaving holes at the front and back for the head, tail, and legs.

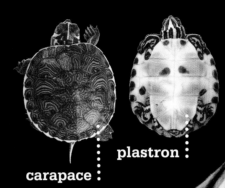

**carapace**

**plastron**

*A turtle moves its head and legs when it breathes, which helps it gulp air.*

**stomach**

**heart**

## The body

A turtle is born with a soft shell. It hardens as it grows, and it continues to grow until the turtle is an adult. All the turtle's organs lie under its shell. Some turtles can also tuck their heads in for defense.

*The heart pumps blood around the body. Blood passes close to the carapace to help it heat up.*

**Some turtles have hinges on their plastrons that can**

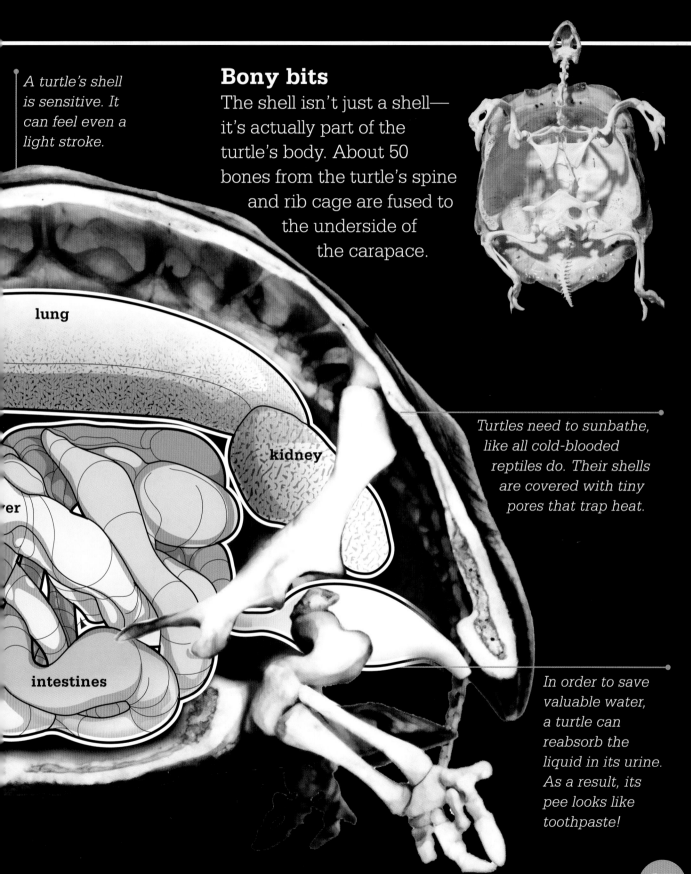

*A turtle's shell is sensitive. It can feel even a light stroke.*

## Bony bits

The shell isn't just a shell—it's actually part of the turtle's body. About 50 bones from the turtle's spine and rib cage are fused to the underside of the carapace.

lung

kidney

er

intestines

*Turtles need to sunbathe, like all cold-blooded reptiles do. Their shells are covered with tiny pores that trap heat.*

*In order to save valuable water, a turtle can reabsorb the liquid in its urine. As a result, its pee looks like toothpaste!*

snap the head holes shut when all body parts are inside

# Shell collection

A turtle's shell reflects its daily life. A high-domed shell protects a turtle from predators; a flat shell helps a turtle swim fast.

green turtle

stinkpot turtle

Florida softshell turtle

Maracaibo wood turtle

East African black mud turtle

gopher tortoise

African spurred tortoise

Indian star tortoise

diamondback terrapin

Galápagos giant tortoise

painted turtle

yellow-bellied slider

pancake tortoise

spotted turtle

Southeast Asian box turtle

yellow-bellied slider

Hermann's tortoise

matamata

olive ridley turtle

leopard tortoise

black-knobbed map turtle

yellow-spotted Amazon river turtle

Aldabra giant tortoise

southern painted turtle

Blanding's turtle

Californian desert tortoise

Barbour's map turtle

alligator snapping turtle

box turtle

diamondback terrapin

# Sea turtles

There are seven species of sea turtle. They live all over the world, in all of the oceans except the Arctic.

**green turtle**

**flatback turtle**

## Endangered seven

All types of sea turtle are either endangered or vulnerable. A big danger is being caught in fishing nets.

## Speedy giant

The leatherback can be as heavy as a cow, but it's quick! It can swim at 15 mph (24 kph), which is as fast as a dolphin.

leatherback turtle

*Sea turtles cry very salty tears. This rids their bodies of salt from the seawater that they drink.*

**A sea turtle's favorite**

hawksbill turtle

Kemp's ridley turtle

leatherback turtle

olive ridley turtle

loggerhead turtle

## Cleaning station

Green turtles visit "cleaning stations," where they are cleaned by fish. Clean shells keep turtles healthy and help them swim more easily. The fish get an easy meal!

green turtle

*The green turtle can hold its breath for five hours!*

*Groups of fish nibble off the algae and parasites that attach themselves to turtle shells.*

## Flippers

Sea turtles' legs are shaped like flippers, so they are powerful and graceful swimmers. Turtles also use their flippers to drag themselves across land.

▶▶▶ **Find out more**
about nesting turtles on the next two pages.

**69**

foods are jellyfish, algae, sea snails, and sponges.

# The life of

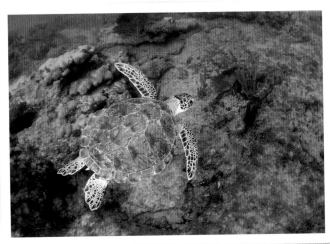

## 1 Beginning the journey

Loggerhead turtles spend their lives at sea. But every two to three years, after mating, the female returns to the beach where she was born to lay her eggs.

## 2 Back to the beach

The female sometimes travels thousands of miles to reach her beach. Nobody knows how she finds her way.

## 5 Back to the sea

She scrapes sand over the eggs to cover them. They will lie safely underground until they hatch. The mother returns to the sea, making tracks in the sand.

## 6 Digging babies

After about 60 days, the baby turtles hatch and dig up through the sand. They wait just beneath the surface until nightfall.

**Many baby turtles never make it to adulthood because**

# the loggerhead turtle

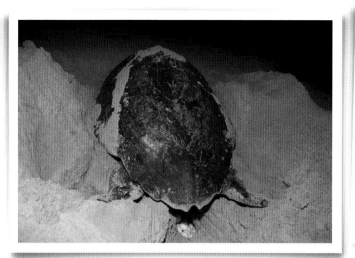

### 3 Finding a good spot
When she reaches land, she uses her front flippers to travel across the sand and her back flippers to dig a nesting hole.

### 4 Laying the eggs
The mother positions herself so that her eggs fall gently into the hole as she lays them. She may lay up to four batches of eggs per season.

### 7 Scramble to the sea
As darkness falls, the babies pop up out of the sand and scramble toward the ocean, heading for the bright horizon over the sea.

### 8 Watch out!
The journey from nest to sea is a dangerous one. Some babies may fall prey to predators like crabs, especially if they are still traveling at dawn.

**of predators—including human turtle-egg poachers.**

# Save the sea turtle

## Over the last 50 years, sea turtle numbers have declined. This is mainly because their nesting beaches are under threat from construction and tourism.

## Leatherback numbers

One of the most affected species of sea turtle is the leatherback. In 1982, there were approximately 115,000 adult female leatherbacks in the world. In 1996, there were as few as 20,000. Soon they may be gone forever.

## How are we

**BRIGHT LIGHTS**

When baby turtles hatch, they head toward the light of the horizon, which is the sea. Building lights confuse them.

Conservationists tag turtles to track their movements. The longest recorded journey was by a leatherback that traveled 12,774 miles (20,558 km) from Indonesia to its breeding ground in Oregon.

leatherback turtle

**Around 25 percent of the crocodiles in the world are**

# endangering sea turtles?

## FISHING

Hundreds of sea turtles are accidentally caught in fishing nets, then drown because they cannot get to the surface to breathe.

## POACHING

In many countries, people steal turtle eggs to sell as food or to collectors. Eggs are easy to poach because turtles abandon them.

## POLLUTION

Sea turtles mistake floating plastic bags for jellyfish, which they like to eat. Turtles choke on the plastic and die.

### spot the difference

Jellyfish . . .        . . . or plastic bag?

# What can you do to help?

## FIND OUT

Conservation charities such as the Sea Turtle Conservancy work to

protect sea turtles around the world. They organize volunteers who want to help; for example, some patrol turtle nesting beaches to protect the eggs from poachers. Check out their website.

## DON'T BUY

Don't buy any reptile products unless you know that they are from a legal and trustworthy supplier.

snakeskin boot

**also under threat. They are killed for their skins.**

# Interview with a

**Name:** Steve Backshall
**Profession:** Explorer, author, host of a wildlife show, and reptile enthusiast

**Q** **Did you like reptiles as a child?**

**A** I would say I was obsessed with them. I remember as a toddler catching lizards on family vacations, finding grass snakes in our manure heap, and learning all the facts I could about mambas and anacondas.

**Q** **What's the best thing about being an explorer?**

**A** Every day is different. I could open my tent door to the Himalayas, the jungle, or the desert— although I don't usually bother with a tent in the desert!

Komodo dragon

**Q** **Where is the best place for reptile spotting?**

**A** On the Baja peninsula of Mexico, I found four species of rattlesnake in one night. But for pure numbers, it's the mass nesting spectacle of olive ridley turtles on the Pacific coast of Costa Rica.

**Q** **What is the weirdest reptile you've seen?**

**A** Probably the elephant trunk snake, which lives in mangroves in the Asian tropics. It has odd, loose skin that looks too big for its body.

**Never touch a snake unless you are 100 percent sure**

# wildlife explorer

**Q** Many people are scared of snakes. Are these reptiles misunderstood?

**A** Definitely. The only people who are really at risk are those who work barefoot in fields and can't get to a hospital. That said, venomous snakes are very dangerous, so don't pick them up!

**Q** Do you ever feel frightened with reptiles?

**A** Yes, but it is important to hide the fear—animals can sense it, and it can make you tense. With experience, you learn how to keep your cool and when you should beat a hasty retreat!

•••••• **king cobra**

**Q** Would you be more nervous about upsetting a king cobra or a Komodo dragon?

**A** I'd try not to upset either of them! I caught a 13-foot-long (4 m) king cobra once, which was pretty crazy. I've also seen Komodos turn from slumbering statues to predatory dinosaurs in a millisecond.

**Q** Has a reptile injured you?

**A** I get lots of nips and scratches. The only substantial bite was from a spectacled caiman I stepped on accidentally. Ten stitches to my leg, but I was back snake hunting the next day!

**Q** If you could be any species of reptile, which would it be?

**A** That's a tricky one! Maybe a leatherback turtle. They have special mechanisms that allow them to keep moving all the time. Mind you, a diet of jellyfish . . . hmm!

what it is!

# Glossary

**ambush**
To attack prey by surprise. A reptile may hide in a burrow, waiting for prey to pass and then attacking.

**antivenin**
A substance that negates the effect of venom. An injection of antivenin can save your life if you are bitten by a venomous snake.

**bask**
To warm one's body in sunlight.

**burrow**
A hole in the ground, made or used by an animal for shelter.

**camouflage**
Natural coloring that helps animals blend in with their surroundings.

**carapace**
The top half of a turtle's shell, covering the turtle's back.

**carnivore**
An animal or plant that eats meat.

**cold-blooded**
Unable to regulate body temperature. Reptiles are cold-blooded and need sunlight to warm themselves up.

**colubrid**
A type of snake, such as a garter snake, that is usually nonvenomous.

**constrictor**
A type of snake that squeezes its prey to death.

**crocodilian**
A category of reptile that includes crocodiles, alligators, and gharials. Crocodilians are large, with long jaws and tails.

**elapid**
A type of venomous snake with fixed fangs, such as a mamba.

**endangered**
At risk of dying out, usually because of human activity.

**fixed fang**
A snake fang that does not move, unlike a hinged fang.

**habitat**
The place or type of place where an animal usually lives and grows.

**hibernate**
To spend the winter in a deep sleep or sleeplike state.

**hinged fang**
A fang that usually lies flat against the roof of a snake's mouth, swinging forward only when the snake strikes. A hinged fang is hollow, and venom can flow through it.

**Jacobson's organ**
A organ on the roof of a snake's mouth that interprets chemical messages from air particles.

**keratin**
The flexible material that fingernails and reptile scales are made of.

**plastron**
The bottom half of a turtle's shell, covering the turtle's underbelly.

**predator**
An animal that hunts and eats other animals.

**prey**
An animal that is hunted and eaten by another animal.

**scale**
One of many protective plates that cover a reptile's skin.

**scute**
One of many tough, bony, platelike scales that cover a crocodilian's skin and make up a turtle's shell.

**turtle**
A category of reptile that includes tortoises (land turtles), sea turtles, and terrapins (turtles that can live both on land and at sea).

**venom**
Poison, used to kill prey. Venom can be milked from snakes for research in medicine.

**vertebra**
One of many bony segments that make up an animal's backbone. The plural of *vertebra* is *vertebrae*.

**viper**
A type of venomous snake with hinged fangs, such as a rattlesnake.

**warm-blooded**
Able to regulate body temperature. Humans are warm-blooded.

*This newly hatched corn snake is about 5 inches (13 cm) at birth but will grow to 6 feet (1.8 m) by adulthood.*

# Index

*This beautifully patterned Chinese stripe-necked turtle lives in ponds, marshes, and streams in China and Vietnam.*

# Thank you


### Interior

1: Masa Ushioda/age fotostock/SuperStock; 2–3 (background), 2tr: iStockphoto; 3tr: Trevor Kelly/Shutterstock; 4–5 (teeth): Eric Isselée/Shutterstock; 4–5 (crocodile in water): Reinhard Dirscherl/Visuals Unlimited, Inc.; 5b: Digital Zoo/Media Bakery; 6–7: Isak Pretorius; 8–9 (background): iStockphoto; 8–9 (chameleon on branch): Chris Doyle/Dreamstime; 8cl: iStockphoto; 8bl: Frans Lanting/Media Bakery; 8bc, 8br: iStockphoto; 9 (scales): Isselee/Dreamstime; 9b: Chawalit Chanpaiboon/Shutterstock; 10–11: Andy Rouse/Getty Images; 10clt: Hugoht/Dreamstime; 10clb: Kevin Schafer/Media Bakery; 10bl: iStockphoto; 11tc: Lorraine Swanson/Dreamstime; 11 (single garter snake): Melinda Fawver/Dreamstime; 11cr: Oscar Dominguez/Alamy; 11br: Arvin C. Diesmos/Associated Press; 12bl: Danihernanz/Getty Images; 12tr: Eric Isselée/Dreamstime; 13 (tail): iStockphoto; 13tl: Isselee/Dreamstime; 13tc: iStockphoto; 13tr: Noam Armonn/Shutterstock; 13bl: iStockphoto; 13br: John Cancalosi/Alamy; 14–15: Solvin Zankl/Visuals Unlimited, Inc.; 16tl: Thinkstock; 16cm: Kevin Walsh/Wikimedia Commons; 16cr: iStockphoto; 16bl: Matt Jeppson/Shutterstock; 16bc: Tjkphotography/Dreamstime; 16br: Trevor Kelly/Shutterstock; 17tl: Ameng Wu/Shutterstock; 17tc: blickwinkel/Alamy; 17tr: Bianca Lavies/National Geographic Stock; 17b: Tjkphotography/Dreamstime; 18 (reticulated python, Komodo dragon): iStockphoto; 18 (Nile crocodile): Eric Isselee/Shutterstock; 18–19: Raul Martin/National Geographic Stock; 20–21 (background, all frames): Ivaylo Ivanov/Shutterstock; 20cl, 20tr: iStockphoto; 20bl: Juniors Bildarchiv/age fotostock; 20bc: Michel Gunther/Science Source; 20–21b: Reinhard Dirscherl/Visuals Unlimited, Inc.; 21tl: Daexto/Dreamstime; 21tr: Bernd Zoller/age fotostock; 21cm: Joe McDonald/Media Bakery; 21cr: Alejandro Sánchez/Wikimedia Commons; 21br: Cathy Keifer/Dreamstime; 22–23: Photoshot Holdings Ltd/Alamy; 24tl: Kendall McMinimy/Getty Images; 24tr: Eric Isselee/Shutterstock; 24–25 (background): iStockphoto; 24–25 (rattlesnake): Martin Harvey/Getty Images; 25tl: iStockphoto; 25tc: Isselee/Dreamstime; 25tr: Eric Isselee/Shutterstock; 26–27t, 26–27b: Isselee/Dreamstime; 27tr, 27br: Mike Garland; 28 (emerald tree boa): Johnbell/Dreamstime; 28 (leopard snake): Michel Gunther/Science Source; 28 (blue coral snake): Chris Mattison/Alamy; 28 (death adder): Gerry Pearce/Alamy; 28 (rainbow boa, carpet python): Amwu/Dreamstime; 28 (brown vine snake): Jack Goldfarb/Media Bakery; 28 (desert horned viper l): blickwinkel/Alamy; 28 (desert horned viper r): Isselee/Dreamstime; 28 (Texas blind snake): Larry Miller/Science Source; 28 (rosy boa): Amwu/Dreamstime; 28 (European grass snake): iStockphoto; 28 (Burmese python): Mikeaubry/Dreamstime; 28 (basilisk rattlesnake): Bernhard Richter/Dreamstime; 28 (eastern king snake): Isselee/Dreamstime; 28 (green vine snake): Geoff Gallice/Wikimedia Commons; 28 (long-nosed tree snake): Fletcher & Baylis/Science Source; 28 (gray-banded king snake): Erllre/Dreamstime; 29 (Pueblan milk snake): Eric Isselee/Shutterstock; 29 (Colorado desert sidewinder): Kcmatt/Dreamstime; 29 (leaf-nosed snake): Alextelford/Wikimedia Commons; 29 (green tree python, Amazon tree boa): Amwu/Dreamstime; 29 (golden flying snake): Sedthachai/Dreamstime; 29 (corn snake, eyelash viper): Isselee/Dreamstime; 29 (saw-scaled viper): Speciestime/Dreamstime; 29 (boa constrictor, snow king snake): Eric Isselee/Shutterstock; 29 (king cobra): Thinkstock; 29 (Gaboon viper): Isselee/Dreamstime; 29 (European adder): Colin Varndell/Photo Researchers, Inc.; 29 (southern copperhead): Isselee/Dreamstime; 29 (green mamba): Mgkuijpers/Dreamstime; 30 (leaves): Lim Yong Hian/Shutterstock; 30 (black mamba): Thinkstock; 30 (young green tree python): fivespots/Shutterstock; 30–31 (background): Christopher Meder/Shutterstock; 30 (golden flying snake): Fletcher & Baylis/Science Source; 30 (flying snakes): Tim Laman/National Geographic Stock; 30 (tree snakes): Svenler/Dreamstime; 31 (ground snakes): Mgkuijpers/Dreamstime; 31 (desert snakes): Bevanward/Dreamstime; 31 (burrowers): Michael & Patricia Fogden/Minden Pictures; 31 (sea snakes): Paul Cowell/Shutterstock; 31 (sidewinder): fivespots/Shutterstock; 31 (rock): Thinkstock; 32t: Steve Bronstein/Getty Images; 32bl: Karl H. Switak/Science Source; 32bc: Heiko Kiera/Shutterstock; 32br: Tom McHugh/Science Source; 33t: Yuri Arcurs/Shutterstock; 33 (ant): iStockphoto; 33bl: Francesco Tomasinelli/Science Source; 33br, 34tl: Joe McDonald/Visuals Unlimited Inc.; 34bl: John Foxx/Thinkstock; 34–35: Digital Vision/Thinkstock; 35tr: Eric Isselee/Shutterstock; 35cl: David Davis/Dreamstime; 35cm: Erllre/Dreamstime; 35cr: Johnbell/Dreamstime; 35br: Heiko Kiera/Shutterstock; 36–37 (background): Mahesh Patil/Shutterstock; 36 (#10): Ryan M. Bolton/Shutterstock; 36 (#8): Dr. Morley Read/Shutterstock; 36 (#4): Tad Arensmeier/Wikimedia Commons; 36 (#1): Andreas Viklund/www.animaldanger.com/Wikimedia Commons; 36–37 (#6): Matthew Cole/Shutterstock; 37 (#7): Mikhail Blajenov/Dreamstime; 37 (#3): Sylvie Lebchek/Shutterstock; 37 (#5): Andre Dobroskok/Shutterstock; 37 (#2): ANT Photo Library/Science Source; 37 (#9): Brooke Whatnall/Dreamstime; 38tl: Philippe Psaila/Science Source; 38tr: Isselee/Dreamstime; 38–39: fivespots/Shutterstock; 39tl: Thinkstock; 39trt: Cathy Keifer/Dreamstime; 39trc: Robert Eastman/Shutterstock; 39trb: Dannyphoto80/Dreamstime; 39c: John Devries/Science Source; 39br: iStockphoto; 40 (Indo-Chinese forest lizard): Bidouze Stéphane/Dreamstime; 40 (Schneider's skink): Mikeaubry/Dreamstime; 40 (green basilisk): JMiks/Shutterstock; 40 (leopard gecko): Branislav Senic/Dreamstime; 40 (veiled chameleon): Lukas Blazek/Dreamstime; 40 (fat-tailed gecko): Amwu/Dreamstime; 40 (flying dragon): Stephen Dalton/Science Source; 40 (blue-tailed skink): Mgkuijpers/Dreamstime; 40 (closed-litter rainbow skink): Jason P Ross/Dreamstime; 40 (lined leaf-tailed gecko): Amwu/Dreamstime; 40 (Komodo dragon): Rico Leffanta/Dreamstime; 40 (green anole): SSilver/Fotolia; 40 (crested gecko): Amwu/Dreamstime; 40 (web-footed gecko): Bevanward/Dreamstime; 40 (European green lizard): Alslutsky/Dreamstime; 40 (Chinese crocodile lizard): Joseph T. & Suzanne L. Collins/Science Source; 40 (agama lizard): Carolyne Pehora/Dreamstime; 40 (broad-headed skink): Melinda Fawver/Dreamstime; 41 (panther chameleon t): Isselee/Dreamstime; 41 (green iguana): Maria Suris/Dreamstime; 41 (emerald monitor): Flame/Alamy; 41 (branch t): John Brueske/Dreamstime; 41 (frilled lizard): Isselee/Dreamstime; 41 (flying dragon): Tom McHugh/Science Source; 41 (blue-tongued skink): Amwu/Dreamstime; 41 (thorny devil): Nick Rains/Alamy; 41 (granite night lizard): Suzanne L. Collins/Science Source; 41 (panther chameleon r): fivespots/Shutterstock; 41 (Jackson's chameleon): Amwu/Dreamstime; 41 (pygmy chameleon): Brandon Alms/Dreamstime; 41 (fire skink, midline knob-tail, Gila monster): Amwu/Dreamstime; 41 (bearded dragon): Alex Bramwell/Dreamstime; 41 (tokay gecko): Timhesterphotography/Dreamstime; 41 (Madagascar day gecko): Eastmanphoto/Dreamstime; 42: Chris Mattison; 42–43 (background and br): Dimitri Vervitsiotis/Media Bakery; 43tl, 43tc: Kasza/Shutterstock; 43tr: Thorsten Negro/Media Bakery; 43cr: iStockphoto; 44tl: Joel Sartore/National Geographic Stock; 44tr: Stephen Dalton/Science Source; 44bl: Doug Plummer/Media Bakery; 44br: Stephen Dalton/Science Source; 45tl: Thinkstock; 45tr: PeterWaters/Dreamstime; 45 (tongue): ladyfoto/Shutterstock; 45bl: USFWS Mountain Prairie; 45br: Claus Meyer/Minden Pictures/Corbis; 46–47 (all): Paul D. Stewart/Science Source; 48tl: Erwin Tecqmenne/Alamy; 48tc: Fletcher & Baylis/Science Source; 48cl: Isselee/Dreamstime; 48bl: fivespots/Shutterstock; 48–49: Pius Lee/Dreamstime; 49t: Tui De Roy/National Geographic Stock/Minden Pictures; 50–51: Thomas Marent; 52–53 (teeth): Eric Isselée/Shutterstock; 52–53 (crocodile in water): Reinhard Dirscherl/Visuals Unlimited, Inc.; 52cl: Eric Isselee/Shutterstock; 52cr: John Kasawa/Shutterstock; 52b: Biophoto Associates/Science Source; 53brt: Asim Bharwani/Wikimedia Commons; 53brc: iStockphoto; 53brb: Thinkstock; 54–55c: Joe McDonald/Visuals Unlimited, Inc.; 55tr: Brenton West/Alamy; 55br: ichbintai/Shutterstock; 56tl: Tony Campbell/Dreamstime; 56tr: Thinkstock; 56cl: Dan Callister/Alamy; 56bl: Dannyphoto80/Dreamstime; 56–57b: Masa Ushioda/age fotostock/SuperStock; 57 (alligator t): Isselee/Dreamstime; 57tl: Jupiterimages/Thinkstock; 57tc: Tony Campbell/Shutterstock; 57tr: UgputuLf SS/Shutterstock; 58t, 58c: iStockphoto; 58bl: James P. Rod/Science Source; 58bc: Robert C. Hermes/Science Source; 58br: Heiko Kiera/Shutterstock; 58–59b: iStockphoto; 59t: C.C. Lockwood/Animals Animals; 59br: Rick Poley/Visuals Unlimited, Inc.; 60–61: Hali Sowle/Getty Images; 61 (Nile crocodile t): Trevor Kelly/Shutterstock; 61tl: Naypong/Shutterstock; 61tc: Dr. P. Marazzi/Science Source; 61tr: Victoria Stone & Mark Deeble/Getty Images; 61cr: Libby Withnall; 61b: Johan Swanepoel/Shutterstock; 62tl, 62cl: iStockphoto; 62–63: Nico Smit/Dreamstime; 63tc: Ryan M. Bolton/Shutterstock; 63rct: Richard Carey/Dreamstime; 63rcm: Jon Stokes/Science Source; 63rcb: Amazon-Images/Alamy; 63br: iStockphoto; 64 (carapace): Shiffti/Dreamstime; 64 (plastron): Ruben Caseiro/Dreamstime; 64–65 (turtle photo): Colin Keates/Getty Images; 64–65 (turtle interior): Mike Garland; 65tr: Steve Vidler/Alamy; 66 (Florida softshell turtle): SuperStock/age fotostock; 66 (Maracaibo wood turtle, stinkpot turtle): fivespots/Shutterstock; 66 (green turtle): Idreamphotos/Dreamstime; 66 (diamondback terrapin): Stephen Bonk/Shutterstock; 66 (African spurred tortoise): iStockphoto; 66 (East African black mud turtle): Eric Isselee/Shutterstock; 66 (gopher tortoise, Indian star tortoise): iStockphoto; 66 (Galápagos giant tortoise): Mikhail Blajenov/Dreamstime; 66 (painted turtle): Jason P Ross/Dreamstime; 66 (yellow-bellied slider): iStockphoto; 66 (pancake tortoise): fivespots/Shutterstock; 66 (spotted turtle, matamata): Joe Blossom/Alamy; 67 (Southeast Asian box turtle): Faizzaki/Dreamstime; 67 (yellow-bellied slider): Birute Vijeikiene/Dreamstime; 67 (olive ridley turtle): Jean2399/Dreamstime; 67 (Hermann's tortoise): INSADCO Photography/Alamy; 67 (leopard tortoise): NatalieJean/Shutterstock; 67 (Aldabra giant tortoise): iStockphoto; 67 (black-knobbed map turtle): Amwu/Dreamstime; 67 (yellow-spotted Amazon river turtle): Sinclair Stammers/Science Source; 67 (southern painted turtle): Michel Gunther/Science Source; 67 (Blanding's turtle): Dennis Donohue/Dreamstime; 67 (Californian desert tortoise): iStockphoto; 67 (Barbour's map turtle): Amwu/Dreamstime; 67 (box turtle): iStockphoto; 67 (diamondback terrapin): Brian Kushner/Dreamstime; 67 (alligator snapping turtle): Faizzaki/Dreamstime; 68l: Scubazoo/Alamy; 68–69 (background and turtle b): idreamphoto/Fotolia; 68tc: iStockphoto; 68tr: William D. Bachman/Science Source; 69tl: Thinkstock; 69tcl: National Park Service/Wikimedia Commons; 69tcm: torsten kuenzlen/Dreamstime; 69tcr: Jason Isley/Scubazoo/Getty Images; 69tr: Michael Ireland/Fotolia; 69c: Tim Davis/Media Bakery; 70tl: Dekanaryas/Shutterstock; 70tr: Michael Ludwig/Dreamstime; 70bl: iStockphoto; 70br: Heiko Kiera/Shutterstock; 71tl: iStockphoto; 71tr: Matt Jeppson/Shutterstock; 71 (baby turtle): Masa Ushioda/Alamy; 71bl: Mitch Reardon/Science Source; 71br: Visual&Written SL/Alamy; 72t: Jim Richardson/Getty Images; 72b: Emily Françoise/Alamy; 73tl: SCUBAZOO/Photo Researchers, Inc.; 73tcl, 73tcr: iStockphoto; 73tr: Win Nondakowit/Fotolia; 73bl: iStockphoto; 73br: Stephen McSweeny/Shutterstock; 74t: Katy Elson; 74b: Sergey Uryadnikov/Shutterstock; 75: iStockphoto; 76–77: Isselee/Dreamstime; 78–79: iStockphoto; 80: Heiko Kiera/Shutterstock.

### Cover

Background: gawrav/iStockphoto. Front cover: (tl) Martin Harvey/Getty Images; (c) Keren Su/Corbis; (bl) Mark Conlin/Getty Images; (br) Eric Isselée/Shutterstock. Spine: Martin Harvey/Getty Images. Back cover: (tr) Thierry Montford/Biosphoto/FLPA; (computer monitor) Manaemedia/Dreamstime.

*This baby python wraps its body around a toad, squeezes it to death, and swallows it whole!*